Poverty's ONE Root Cause

Copyright 2015 by Edward E. Slater, Jr

First Edition

All rights reserved

ISBN 978-1-329-30012-5

Jacket design by T. B. Scarpacci

For Jeanie, Susan, Eddie,
Stephanie, and Nancy, all who
understand love and responsibility,
and for Jack, Rylie, Jered, Xavier,
Zachary, Diego, and August

Preface

"Good morning! Good morning. My name is Fredrick B., and I'm more happy to be here than you could ever imagine. I'll try to prove something about how I feel to be standing here and seeing you...although you remind me of a thousand people at a gladiator fight, waiting for action. And, I forgot my sword. It's kinda' scary, but I have a reason to be here. Actually, I'm compelled to talk to you today. There's something inside that won't let me chicken out. I'll explain it."

In the Maple City High School auditorium there are seats for six hundred students. The seats are the flip-down, formed, lacquered plywood kind that seem comfortable for about ten minutes. In the eleventh minute, the average high schooler starts twisting and sliding around to relieve that itch of boredom or to broadcast his desire to be anywhere else. Whispering and jostling starts like a little ripple, and then it sloshes from aisle to aisle until there's a steady-state of movement like choppy little waves splashing against each other in a Great Lake. From the stage, it's like six hundred synchronized swimmers, all out of time.

"I've had a lifetime to prepare for today, and I'll admit that recently I've practiced at least ten times every day. I hope it shows. I've never wanted to be anywhere or to bring something valuable to someone more in my life. In fact, I'd like to say I'm living for you today."

"Today, February twenty-fourth, is the day I was scheduled to die. It could have been exposure to the cold, malnutrition, or it could have been shame. I got a reprieve, though."

Five hundred and ninety five teenagers turned into silent stone statues. "I gave up thinking about the end. I used to try to sleep with something draped over my head so I could pretend to be anonymous. In my mind I tried to escape from my situation dozens of times, and I had ingenious plans, but for me it was about not enough courage. Who stole my courage, I'd ask, but nobody ever answered."

The auditorium's sea seemed at a dead calm now. Eyes looked forward toward the thin man on the stage. He seemed to hesitate, about to cry. His face drooped, like his pants. Students in the front row perceived Fredrick's shirt to be two sizes too big. As he described his "death row" vision, he seemed to become frail. Smaller. Vulnerable.

But then after silence punctuated by an iconic five second body language display about fragility and regret, Fredrick The Bold figuratively lept back onto the stage and bared his teeth. His bicepts and all the muscles in his legs seemed to swell, and he became a taller figure. A man of steel ready to attack. But, with words.

"My resting place was cardboard on concrete," he blurted in a resolute steel confession. "I lived in a dismal remote place where people came and went, but I never got introduced. I slept in sunshine in order to get warm. I roamed around at night in case an opportunity would find me. I was hungry for long periods of time, separated by little feasts of other people's scraps. Some days, I was able to make it to the "Food Line", where I could line up like a beggar (lining up with other beggars) for a meal made up of food other people didn't want."

"The story about my past is better left in some dusty diary, where my acquaintences stole like thieves and they fought like Coliseum slaves. There would be a chapter on child abuse and one on starvation, one about hatred and one about hopelessness. Humiliation. Surrender. Darkness. But, we're going to leave that book in a secret drawer."

"It's a long story about how I agreed to come here today."

"I don't really remember where I was. I don't remember if it was morning or afternoon. When you don't live in a house, or a car, or a back room, or a basement, or a garage, or a tool shed, or a shanty, or a cave, you spend hours trying to think of the other alternatives, and you lose track of time. I lived on Main Street, Third Street, Wilden Avenue, in "The Hollow", at the Fairgrounds, and at all the parks. I've slept in homeless shelters, abandoned cars, under car ports, behind bushes, in dumpsters, in stair wells, beside the river, and behind every restaurant in town. It's easy to hide in the dark, but it's hard to explain when you're confronted by someone who notices you and thinks you're a criminal. I own some cardboard, blankets, and two tarps. They all roll up into what looks like a paratrooper's pack. I've dreamed of being a paratrooper, but...well."

"So, I'm there at my winter estate near a scenic park beside the river, and this man who looks like a police detective comes straight for me. But, he looked too old to give me a chase, so I wasn't too worried. I thought he might have eyed my paratrooper's pack, so I worked the strap around my shoulder and held on. He looked straight at me and challenged me with an insane idea about giving a speech to some high schoolers."

"He said, "Let's go get a hamburger and talk.""

"We're standing out there in Pumpernickel Park between the picnic pavilion and a big bed of sticker-tipped holly bushes, and I'm pretty curious about this whole crazy idea. But, I'm hungry, too. He invited me to follow him across the avenue to a pretty good place to eat. We ate hot food."

"I thought a lot about things like second chances and opportunities. I thought about courage and redemption. I tried to figure out where my dignity was buried. I wondered who would care."

Fredrick started to pace back and forth on the auditorium stage in order to keep some of the kids from going to sleep.

"Heck, I'm available, I thought. I'm overdue for doing something to prop up my life. Why not poke failure in its good eye? What I signed up for was to give a speech to six hundred teenagers at the High School...to come up with a forty minute lecture. I could tell my own story about my first hand experience. I could tell where I sleep and where I eat. I could tell about today."

"Then I thought I should think this through. Oh heck, it's stupid to think of me making a fool of myself. But if it's ever going to end...maybe this is how to begin my major overhaul to be someone."

"I was reminded that I'm not being asked to be a teacher, I'm a guest speaker. I'm an expert in my field. I'm a citizen from the community who has something to say, and this is my 40 minutes to say it. I don't know whether I want my brain to take over or my heart to speak. I guess I could be planting seeds that prevent homelessness and poverty for 600 youngsters. I'll bet I can do this."

"Both my parents were MIA twenty-three hours a day, and I didn't have any perceptions about how to be someone. I knew how to be *nobody*, though. I could hide out, and I could go to school, but I wasn't a priority on any list, so the world swallowed me, keeping it all a secret."

"If you're living a secret life without a priority, I'm telling you right now to bust out and take control of your life. I'm going to give you the Freshman course. What if you want to be an architect, surgeon, air traffic controller, emergency medical technician, a great parent, or anyone else who takes lives in their hands...anyone who protects the good things and prevents the bad things. Here's your cue: you're going to be known for your courage, your confidence, and your skill in making decisions. You can make the connection right here today, and you'll be twenty years ahead of where I was at sixteen years old."

"When a situation arises, go ahead and step up, step in, and take charge. For most circumstances, someone needs to take charge even if it's to convince others things are under control. How do I know? My parents moved around a lot. Sometimes, I didn't know the address. I was lucky to find my way to a sleeping place some days. If nobody takes charge, it's up to you. Somebody has to be in charge of your well being, and someday it's going to be you. If nobody is in charge of being there for you today, come see me. Now, I know where there's help for teenagers."

"There are five kinds of personal responsibility that I had never heard about until a couple of months ago. I never got the message about *wasteful behaviors*, but I did them all. Alcohol, drugs, gambling, lying, stealing, lewdness. I was abused, I was lazy, arrogant, selfish, hateful, and I wanted to get revenge. Figure out how to say *no* to those despicable things. Have courage. If you will find me later, I can help."

"Do you mow the grass or baby-sit? Do you volunteer to wash the windows or the pots and pans? Do you have the guts or the brains to clean up your room and hang up you clothes? Well, at some point, you'll find out the easy way or the hard way that *honest hard work* is your best friend. There's a lot of dignity in honest hard work, even as a teenager."

"I'm going to make you a promise. I promise you that if you contact me for advice or moral support, I'll be there for you. In fact, I want you to try me. And, if you make *me* a promise, I'll want you to come through, too. I'll expect it, and you'll find there are really important people in your futures who will expect you to come through. The mortgage company, the credit card company, your boss, your spouse. Everyone who gets a promise from you deserves your honest effort to come through."

"If you think your high school diploma or your college degree qualifies you for Easy Street, you're wrong. The world and the 6 billion inhabitants are quick change artists. Businesses change, processes improve, people shift and adjust to lighten the load and accomplish the max. Some people are out there ready to steal you blind. Your role is to keep a lookout and learn from as many places as possible. As an adult, you'll find that lots of lessons are essentially free. You'll learn more from your neighbors, friends, and work mates than you suspect. Always be ready. Your value to your family, your employer, and your community will grow. And, you'll be an indirect beneficiary, too. Then, pass it on to your children and grandchildren."

"There will be greater priorities, and there will be lesser priorities. I'm now an expert in this. The highest priority in your lifetime will be the children who depend on you for everything. They're vulnerable. Their memories (and their laptop hard drives) don't have much data accumulated. It's up to you to fill their default modes with experiences, pictures, and stories. Every child needs his or her parents' care to neutralize the anxieties and fears that sap their happiness. They need you to care. Your children (this is my very highly experienced opinion) need to be your number one priority. When your kids are in high school and beyond, you'll look back on all your sacrifices and honest hard work that kept them safe, and you'll be warm all over. Then you'll understand self esteem."

"The reason I know all this is because a few months ago I was freezing out under the pavilion shelter at Pumpernickel Park, and today I'm warm all over. Your kind attention and the opportunity to give you this lesson about life's decisions made it possible."

"I'm personally responsible for everything I've said."

"Thank you for listening."

Author's Note

I didn't go out in February to Pumpernickel Park trying find some random homeless person who would help me light the fuse to incinerate poverty. I went to enlist a firecracker with front line experience to tell about. I was a student at Maple City High School in the 1950s, and I attended one class with Fredrick Barbaugh's firecracker father, Gerald. My memory of "Jerry" Barbaugh had to do with one assignment in Speech class, where he gave a two minute speech I'll never forget. He began his speech on "One of the Most

Memorable Moments of My Life" by admitting that he "killed a man". Nobody remembered the other minute and fifty-eight seconds of his speech. I've always wondered if Jerry was trying to give us heart attacks or just putting some shock impact in "memorable". He certainly accomplished the shock.

I knew about the Barbaughs too, because the Maple City News was eager for any story off the police blotter, and the Barbaugh family got frequent bad publicity. Trouble with the Barbaugh parents was in the small print more than once. It was no surprise that Freddy had trouble crossing the bridge to adulthood, but it wasn't a complete surprise that he had the "stuff" to do what his Dad did in Speech class fifty-five years ago. Freddy was fantastic doing what he was called to do because someone cared about him and six hundred people gave him their attention.

Today, Fredrick Barbaugh is a chauffeur for a transportation (limousine) company, and he drives travelers to and from airports in Fort Wayne, South Bend, Indianapolis, and Chicago. On slow days, Freddy's Town Car is parked at the Maple City Boys Club, where he's a volunteer. He seems to have unlimited energy now that he's made the decision to let his new self esteem and courage take him places. He has spoken to school assemblies in eighteen different high schools.

Poverty's One Root Cause

Poverty's One Root Cause

> *Every pointless hour spent, every word uttered in hatred, every surrender of hope, and every waste of substance absorbs and muffles the unimaginable energy God generated on our behalf eleven billion years ago.*
>
> *And, there is poverty.*

Poverty's One Root Cause

Contents

....	Introduction
Chapter 1............	Poverty Defined
Chapter 2............	Maybe "Poverty" isn't Really Poverty
Chapter 3............	Dictating and Judging Lifestyles
Chapter 4............	Building and Destroying
Chapter 5............	Poverty's Table of Elements
Chapter 6............	Education and Poverty
Chapter 7............	Poverty and Capitalism
Chapter 8............	By Example
Chapter 9............	Instinct, Intuition, Psychology
Chapter 10..........	Poverty and Income Inequality
Chapter 11..........	Caution
Chapter 12..........	Swiss Cheese
Chapter 13..........	Morality and Poverty
Chapter 14..........	Handy and Rose
Chapter 15..........	Diluting Responsibility
Chapter 16..........	Teaching Personal Responsibility
Chapter 17..........	Coffee at Jasper's
Chapter 18..........	Dean Ocean (O'Shay), Reno, Nevada
Chapter 19..........	Saying "No" to Poverty
Chapter 20..........	Other Effects of the "One Cause" Claim
Chapter 21..........	Popular Solutions to Poverty
Chapter 22..........	The Wrong Answers
....	Conclusions
....	Letter to County Welfare Board
....	Signatures of Personal Responsibility
....	Thank You

Poverty's One Root Cause

Introduction

Poverty will never escape the realities and fears of human civilization. There will always be impoverishment of the weak and unaware, and there will be voluntary poverty for those counter culture self prescribers whose socio-introverted lifestyles tend to cloud the crystal ball paradise-seekers seek to clear up. There will be freedom and there will be squanders of freedom's subsets by citizens who fail to prioritize and toil for the rights they were born to inherit from generations who did not fail.

Someday, poverty will be proven by social geneologists to have a close kinship to both addiction and slavery, and rigorous definitions of both will expose the kevlar links. Poverty and its peer travesties will be found to be solvable as effects, not causes. The yardstick of measurement in this book will be based on axioms extracted from moral objective principles. We will deduce together through poverty stricken clutter and selfish advocacies to find crystal ball clarity. If we can't eradicate poverty tomorrow, let's at least try to understand poverty's demons today.

We'll examine what is and what is not. We'll catalog the known and we'll worry about the unknown. For every conclusion, we'll try to paste an explanatory note with provenance and ancestry so as to assist (or counteract) those who would seek to critique.

Why search for poverty's one root cause? To solve the problem of poverty and knock it out of the park, of course. Oh yes, we could use the shotgun. We could attack one chunk of the problem at a time, like alcoholism, and we might make a dent in poverty. Or, winning the war on drugs would surely diminish the effects of poverty for millions of impoverished Americans. But track the trillions of dollars, and you'll conclude that's been tried. What about working on greed and selfishness? Would that do it? Where's the will to attack capitalism and elite enterprises, those privileged fountains of favoritism that have been reported to create poverty among less fortunate? Why isn't our crusade against inequality stinging and changing the consciences of more upper middle class citizens? Working on a solution to the run-away sperm donor/father epidemic would make for less poverty among single mothers, but how much long term help would that be when so few of the men involved would care to make changes to their careless lifestyles? Attacking dozens of problems would take forever. Who could be enlisted? Who would pay? Why should we even try to fix something way beyond our limited abilities?

The answer to "why" is not a list nor a litany. The solution is not a series of masks nor an endless loop of exultations. There are individuals who don't want the problem of poverty to be solved, just like there are those who don't want drug business, gambling revenue, alcohol sales, nor commerce in other useless and wasteful (but profitable) endeavors to be limited. But, don't give in. The answer is here. When you get to the chapter where the answer is laid out, let it sink into your mind and give it your best critique. Then, let's get to work out in the field and let's behave like role models who actually want to improve the world. It's up to us. It's useful but often difficult to find the real root cause of a problem. But, finding the root cause is the only rational way to engineer a permanent solution. Often the search for a solution is a hit and miss exercise in chaos and gamesmanship. In an undisciplined approach there are usually lots of "false" causes and dead ends that are unhelpful. These useless avenues sometimes are offered by the guilty to mask their own culpability, and sometimes there are solutions offered by "guessers" in attempts to play hero. Sometimes a random stab at a solution might just work. Usually, though, random stabs just waste time and provide bottomless money pits. If we're going to fix anything, we have to know as much as can be known. It will take diligence, patience, persistence, and hard work.

We could be fixing a coffee maker, or we could be fixing poverty. The same principles apply. We'll have to dissect the bowels of the problem and try to understand how each component plays its role. We'll try to strip away opinions from facts. We'll test every reasonable theory that could explain poverty, and we'll see what fits. Then, we'll critique all the possibilities to make sure we've found the lowest common denominator. The root cause of poverty is the one cause that, if neutralized, will pave the way to eradicating culture-specific poverty.

Poverty's One Root Cause

Chapter 1...........................Poverty Defined

Our Federal definition of "poverty level" uses a yardstick that's based on the dollar value of a demographically adjusted basket of goods. Poverty then is the dollar income for individuals and families that is at or below the Federal poverty level. So, you're in poverty if your income doesn't measure up to the amount the government thinks it ought to. Items in the basket of goods are selected by the government, but your income is (pretty much) selected by you. If you think you are not personally responsible for your notch on the yardstick, read on.

The government gets a B+ for trying to quantify a quality of life metric that tempts us to give assistance to citizens unable to "make it". My definition is similar, but it helps me divine the causes (and the one root cause) of poverty. I'm calling **culture-specific poverty**, a human condition in which hunger, comfort, safety, personal needs (like clothing and hygiene), or a condition of physical and psychological health are unable to be effectively confronted without assistance. In the United States, the Administrative definition of poverty uses opinions of experts and so does mine, but my expert is often the individual who actually lives his or her unique human condition. For lots of the shortcomings in an impoverished life, money is not the best answer (in some cases, money the wrong answer). Personalized care and kindness are never wrong answers.

Lots of organizations and some highly experienced social groups have constructed their own means of judging and attacking poverty. Some of those non-governmental entities are doing an outstanding job. Those successes are what lead me to believe that by defining poverty in terms of an income level and fixing it with other people's money is a short-sighted (and frankly, a lazy) way out. You should agree that most "one size fits all" solutions leave something on the table, usually effective results. The federal definition takes a one size fits all assumption of what poverty is and applies it to anyone who can stretch to fit in. Hundreds of thousands of Americans who live in (culturally) impoverished conditions unable to make their incomes stretch to fit their lifestyles cannot make use of a poverty claim. Millions of citizens live happily with meager incomes and tap your tax money hidden within the 139 Federal welfare programs for larger shares.

Luckily, finding and fixing the root cause of poverty, whether we define "poverty" as a family income level, or whether we define it more accurately as a condition much more complicated than the simplistic Federal yardstick, is a job we can do. The fix for poverty defined as an income level is money. Pulling families up above the poverty line is easy in a social construct where (lots of) individuals contribute willingly to others (a few) who are truly and obviously in need of the things money can buy. But, the simple yardstick in a complex arena fails. It's not even a matter of "measure twice, fix once," it's "get a different yardstick."

Except for the aged and incapacitated, the words "truly and obviously needy" has a temporary flavor. Help for the aged and incapacitated is help a grateful society ought to be able to compassionately provide as a humanitarian duty. Reasonably fit citizens who need a step up to self-sufficiency ought to be assisted by community professionals answering to a caring local population. Self-sufficiency is the key, though, and overcoming a broken link in the chain of experience, knowledge, and wisdom can take the form of an extraordinary personalized intervention.

Chapter 2............Maybe "Poverty" Isn't Really Poverty

Can a family of 4 survive on an annual earned income of $23,850? Let's not risk drowning in a pool of opinions, because advocates both rational and irrational have their opinions smeared across every scrolling media marquee and headline. Unfortunately, poverty (as in "not enough money") is a rallying cry for people who think they don't have enough money or simply want more of anything that's free. The truth is that lots of Americans live just fine with incomes below the official poverty line. Others would be living poverty-stricken lifestyles even if their incomes were twice the Federal threshold. Motivators (like the possibility of a monthly check) spark large quantities of ingenuity and then the proponents come out of the woodwork. If I could find a quarter of a million families that live just fine on modest incomes (many below the poverty line), would that be meaningful? I can do it. I can show you a low income collection of families living simply, with the knowledge and ability to supplement their own diets with fresh organic produce, socialize together, sing together, learn, and pray. And, the 250 thousand contented Americans I'm talking about aren't asking for welfare. They're healthy and vibrant because they get up with the chickens (literally) and go to bed when the sun fades. Every adult works more than 8 hours every day, and each could survive for months on inventories of stockpiled food. These are Americans who don't buy useless products and they don't pay interest, because they don't borrow. The homes and properties of these exemplary civilians are simple, adequate, neat, and clean. They're happy, and they'd be embarrassed to beg for money they didn't earn. They maintain savings for emergencies and most are probably wealthier (with farms, livestock, and modest machinery) than 50 percent of all Americans. The Amish live simply without shame. And, here's something else, lots of Amish families have more children than you have. The children are loved and cared for, and they're educated in real school programs that meet Federal standards. Amish families honor their parents and grandparents. They build their futures on knowledge assembled from decades of experience that they unselfishly share. Generations know what nature has to offer, and they know what works and what doesn't work. Amish communities have learned that both cooperation and kindness pay off. There's a common understanding that moral principles guide humans who respect a higher power to higher callings. Those principles direct the people to live useful lives, and they lead the Amish to believe it's unlikely that poverty can exist in a honest, hard working, loving community. An artificially contrived income level that's below or above the Federal poverty threshold just doesn't matter. How's that for evidence? Can you take tips from the Amish and leverage that information to benefit your family? Of course you can. Even without the bonnet, buggy, and beard.

If you can't think of alternatives to paying for the high costs of taxis and cars, and if your mortgage payment (or rent) eats up way too much on payday, maybe you need some cost cutting lessons. Maybe you should let up on your obsession with the granite counter top and the half acre dog run. If your diet is mostly food prepared by others, you're missing out on some wonderful, stay-at-home, learn-to-cook-it-yourself meals. If your lifestyle fits your income, you can still be happy.

Chapter 3.................Dictating and Judging Lifestyles

Could we describe poverty, its effects, its cause, and its cure without judging the people in our population pool? Is it reasonable to define what "starving" means for other people? Is there a type of house that qualifies for "above the level of poverty" and a lesser one that means the occupants are "impoverished?" Would a peek inside someone's closet reveal a citizen's yes/no ranking for poverty entitlements? Can an administrative branch use those factors to sort individuals and families into poverty categories? Does a young man who spends every dollar on drugs deserve the taxpayers' assistance when he cannot pay for milk and diapers at the grocery store? Will you help the able bodied citizen who will not help himself with the bothersome task of looking for work?

Are there fair judges of "adequate" housing, and are there wise people within our culture capable of analyzing the ifs and thens of who is able to live there? Does your state and community have climatic or geographic characteristics that make it unreasonably difficult to live comfortably? Where is that threshold of "comfort" that separates the people in poverty from the rest? Is the food in your pantry adequate to supply "good enough" nutrition? How healthy is "healthy enough"? Have you been taking good care of yourself? Or, are you having a personal stewardship issue?

These questions mattered to the bureaucrats who set $23,850 per year for a family of 4 as the threshold of poverty. They averaged you in with other people who may be living extraordinarily different lifestyles in different remote or urban settings, with or without a water supply, with or without a supermarket nearby, and with or without a space for chickens and a milk cow.

How did they do it? Think that through.

In order to make our humanitarian mark on the poverty question, we have a choice to make about helping others who are unable to help themselves. I know there are deserving handicapped or disabled folks to assist, and occasionally we come upon a citizen in distress, a victim of the unmanageable, accidental, unpredictable, or worse.

But, there are some citizens who might not deserve a lift out of their reasonably manageable situations. When you create your own definition of poverty, a generous spin might give you a flash of pride to be of service to the needy. I've certainly done it. But you might be doing a disservice. In fact, charity often runs the risk of doing harm rather than good.

I worked at a little job, and I got a payday. I've (luckily) been capable of tweaking my lifestyle to fit my income from savings and sacrifices I made many years ago, and I don't mind living modestly. I drink tap water instead of Starbucks, and lots of my meals are makeshift right off the carbohydrate shelf. My old car could easily be a bicycle, and my clothes would be just fine even if they were off the size 36 rack at Goodwill.

I'm driven to waste-not. I try hard to not throw away good water, food, electricity, fuel, opportunities, friendships, nor good information. I fight to subdue wasteful temptations, and It's been the fourteenth round before I subdued one or two. I'm thankful for the little I've got because for most everything I have, I worked hard for it. Could you judge where to mark my notch the poverty yardstick? I'd really prefer to do it myself.

Chapter 4......................Building and Destroying

We're the sum total of all the likes and dislikes, the biases, and the deeply held beliefs that got stacked one on another over previous ancestral generations. Although I look like my grandmother, I catch myself trying to act like my stepfather, whose respectability I revered. I know my default modes were shaped and taught to me (sometimes without a word spoken) by parents and grandparents who learned from their parents and grandparents. Your family values (and those of most of us) have been built and sharpened over perhaps hundreds of years. Dynasties have been built like bridges spanning those centuries. So, we are what people before us were, a composition of layers and a sum total.

But, what happens to a bridge that fails, falling into the fast flowing river or the ebbing sea? That land route to the other side is gone, not to be quickly reconnected, and no longer commanding the same sense of reliability. Sometimes, a fallen bridge is just too costly to repair or rebuild, and it's abandoned. The same is true for families. One link in the chain of family history failing due to factors (like addiction, death, divorce, or financial debacle) that destroy succession of quality attributes and values usually ends a dynasty. A new sequence of family ascendancy that starts at zero has to acquire all those lessons about "what to do" and "how to do it" and "why" all over again.

It's no wonder, then, that marriages torn apart by divorce, with children adrift and with no connection to the family past are like the failed bridge. And, it's not surprising that the fresh start involved in trying to weld infrastructures of food and shelter and survival back together is rocky. How does a teenager recover his or her sense of the family history after being abandoned by a parent? How does a young couple judge the risks of marriage when they're short changed by empty boxes on the checklist of emotional assets or without a dowry of love and experiential gold from Mama and Dad?

My definition of poverty (and poverty's solution) has to include those assets that come from generations of family whose contributions of valuable intangibles are either there in the cedar chest or they are missing. So, for me, poverty isn't much about money. Poverty is about whether or not those life support assets that have deep roots in family history are available.

Poverty is not often about robbery, but more often about throwing away. It's about abandonment and giving up. It's about bowing to those raw instincts that were not repaired and polished during evenings around the dinner table while Uncle Bud told about the year Mabel made him quit playing minor league baseball. It's about missing the lesson about the pilot who got shot down...at home. It's about giving up the chance to listen to corny jokes and watch some stupid TV show with your brother. Poverty is born to self-prescribed victims and to quitters. Poverty sneaks into homes where love gets mortgaged in order to buy some worthless idea or piece of junk. Poverty is a convenient crack filler that gets patched into holes where grandma's principles of morality used to be.

Chapter 5....................Poverty's Table of Elements

Poverty is a condition of the human living situation. Does the individual have a place for safekeeping a supply of food and water? Is there enough food for today and tomorrow? Is there a shelter that keeps out the wind and rain and snow? Are conditions (like warmth) able to be kept at healthy and safe levels? Are there clothes and shoes sufficient for health and safety? Does the space contain a place for restful sleep? Is there a social element sufficient to prevent psychological distress from both anxiety and loneliness. Is there a lifestyle guide, like a family album of life's lessons there on the shelf? Was it written by forefathers who cared for your well being, and did it depict histories of behaviors and consequences, of both failing and succeeding? If it is unreasonably difficult for an individual to maintain the sovereignty and condition of his or her haven, then that individual unable to perform or contract out the maintenance job is truly "impoverished", and my definition of poverty has been met.

Poverty cannot be defined as a condition that triggers an entitlement of (taxpayer) assistance for you to live in a three bedroom home just so yours will be similar to the other homes in your neighborhood. What other people have has no bearing on your condition. I reject the "community standards" argument that claims low income residents are entitled to receive supplements so they can live in homes like others in their residential locale. A threshold of poverty cannot exist simply because a person chooses to live in a specific town or neighborhood. Americans can be very mobile, so moving to another neighborhood, town, or state should be an alternative solution.

Poverty cannot be defined in terms of income relative to a bureaucratically engineered "threshold" where administrative adjustments are made via tax policy. No citizen who earns wages above the threshold agrees to having his pay "taken away" without at least an internal struggle, and no citizen below threshold income should vote for getting free money (without an internal struggle). Redistribution as a part of a culture using socialistic political structure has never survived in the history of the world. Usurpation of wages in a "free" culture to be redistributed to others is a paradoxical idea destined to fail. The fact is that unilateral redistribution is only a bait to attract potential recipients to the hook of subservience (that's another essay). I believe every American who can reasonably work at some meaningful job earning a regular income can arrange his or her lifestyle so as to sustain a personal stock of subsistence and housing. I'm sure we (Americans) have the ingenuity to design anti-poverty situations that fit almost any lifestyle. Also, that same inventive spirit ought to be able to find or build opportunities enabling individuals to optimize their usefulness in the labor pool and then qualify for higher paying jobs.

Able bodied adults who stay at home waiting for specific high end job offers need to be encouraged to return to the job market in a different career slot (one that is actually available). Encouragement should come directly and indirectly from the taxpayers. The indirect method should involve contraction of current lengthy unemployment benefits. Disincentives work just as effectively as incentives. Continuing for weeks and years to pay out of work citizens who choose to stay at home is their incentive to shun work, and the incentive needs to be dismantled. Why do I have such a stingy attitude about sending people back to work in jobs that may have a lower pay scale? Why such a judgmental sounding idea? Because "honest hard work" exemplifies something right and moral. Working at a useful job is better (financially and morally) than not working at any job.

Chapter 6......................Education and Poverty

The cycle of "poor educations beget poverty" and "poverty begets poor educations" will whirl around in an endless loop until we give both DNA examinations and determine paternity. Luckily, I'm convinced that throwing taxpayer's money at both poor education and at poverty just muddies the search for real solutions. Meanwhile, these conclusions make sense to me: (1) Schools in poverty-stricken areas cannot get the strategic tools and assets to compete, so educations suffer, and (2) Poverty has a diminished chance of being solved when residents lack basic educations.

I am not saying that uneducated people cause poverty. I'm on this bandwagon that both poverty and lousy educations have the same root cause. It's the failure of (in this case) parents to take personal responsibility for getting excellent educations for their children. Lots of parents who fit the Federal definition of poverty succeed in acquiring excellent educations for their children. I know college graduates and extraordinarily successful professionals whose parents fell below the Federal poverty threshold. But, the job of educating those young people got handled through persistence and sacrifice. Those families exemplify what I'm saying about personal responsibility.

Chapter 7......................Poverty and Capitalism

For every winner, there's a loser. Yes, in football and checkers.

For every manufacturer who becomes richer, there are customers who become poorer. Really? Why would customers buy products and knowingly tumble toward poverty? Oh, I see. It's a semantics tumble. Like at the lemonade stand, where Lucy gets 50 cents richer when she sells a cup, and Will gets 50 cents poorer. Conveniently left out is Will's satisfying quench. I'm afraid the richer/poorer argument is from the 3rd grade. It's a reject in the real world.

That elementary try is the same for the employer/worker claim. So the workers suffer payday disasters when they get a paltry paycheck from their 40 hours at the mill? Why come back Monday?

Capital accumulation is a greedy domination trick that corners the market on money so the little guy can't get any. Oh, yeah? Does the little guy have a job? Has someone been drinking the lemonade at Lucy's stand too long?

Some evil capitalists set prices too high. Sometimes, they jack up prices just when people seem to need products the most. Ultimately, only rich people can afford the good stuff. What's that called? Favoritism? Class discrimination? I call it jealousy. It's resentment and envy. The truth is that freedom to compete opens the window of opportunity so any individual or cooperative can get into the same business (and probably do it better). Is the connection to poverty in an inability to work and earn? To maintain a haven of shelter and comfort? Does this price fix make food unavailable or limit nutrition? Is there something that cuts off social interaction? What about health care? Did the Emergency Room close due to capitalism? No, no, no, no, no.

Those darn capitalists want to grow everything bigger. Profit, production, customer base, market share, sales zones, gross sales, everything but wages. But, those darn capitalists thrive on competition, and you do, too. Surprised?

The reason your wages are at the current level is that the value of your particular skill and experience is on a sliding scale. In an area where the supply of labor (like yours) is plentiful, the pay slide moves down until supply and demand are satisfied. In other localities where lots of unfilled jobs are available, your wages will rise until the demand equals supply. Of course, there are other factors that interfere with the demand/supply equilibrium, such as contracts, labor versus management pressures, and government intervention. Capitalism got a bad name in the 19th century, when banks, railroads, oil, and steel were dominated by monopolistic owners, unchecked by a balance of competetive pressures. Wages and prices were at the mercy of individuals who dominated single essential industries. Some of those individuals caused the bad taste being decried today, and even though a century has passed, the "blame capitalism" trick works in neighborhoods where history lessons are light. In those precincts, looking for someone to blame for poverty is an easy, handy, populist pastime.

But, demands for free enterprise, market freedom, and safeguards on competition in the American business culture have won the trust and respect of lots of Western consumers and manufacturers. The century of grace has expired, so the only blamers are people high on envy and low on competitive energy.

Chapter 8..........................By Example

I was on my way to see the "retired" man of the hilly neighborhood. Estil was a dusty thin man who seemed to have a permanent sitting position starched into his frail body. He sat stone still on a rickety porch that was more cracks than boards. I looked at his demeanor constantly as I made my way up past a weather checked post that must have held an old mail box, now deceased. Yellow dirt and stones the size of rice and peas seemed to jump like fleas into my shoes as I leaned and trudged into the sunshine and the swelter.

Estil didn't waste words. "You from the government?" he asked, speaking mostly from his nose.

"No," I replied, with a smile and a hint of breathlessness. "I'm looking for good ideas. I heard that somebody up here figured out how to get along with two apple trees and a goat. I'm interested in learning how to do that."

The old man let his lower lip droop in what I suspected was the start of a friendly grin. In fact, he gave one chuckle and spoke with a little gravel in his voice, "Where ya gittin' the goat?" Then, he curled up his mouth in a big skeptical smile.

I responded right away, "Aw, I'm partial to Amish goats. They eat more, but they give more milk, and they don't kick. What kind you got?"

He just looked to see if his white and cream colored nanny was in view in the side yard. "Sane", he graveled, "She's the best. Betcha she gives more milk than your Amish goat," he said more clearly.

"You've got a sane goat?" He looked me right in the eye and said "Yeah, it's the Sane breed...an' she ain't in no religion."

I decided not to ask what kind of apple trees Estil had, but I saw the two scraggly trees down the hill about a hundred feet from the house. "You got a grocery store around here?" I asked.

"Yeah, but they ain't got no goats," with more gravel this time.

"Ok," I responded, smiling, "Gotta find a grocery store and look for stuff for supper." He's going to make me ask, isn't he? "Which way?"

"Down there, 'bout fittee-two miles," he said, with a really big grin.

I saw that he had perfect teeth, too perfect to be real. "Could I come back and visit after supper, I think I've got a lot to learn."

"Yeah, what you gettin' to eat?"

"I'm thinkin' a couple aspirins and a piece of cheese," I replied. "About a gallon of water."

Abruptly, Estil grabbed the arms of his rocking chair and straightened up to about five foot two. He steadied himself against the porch post and stepped deliberately down off the one step. His bowed legs made a whisking sound as he took a few steps toward me, about 8 feet. "I got that," he offered. "Come on in," and he reached out to shake my hand like we were family.

I said in a low voice, "I'm Ed Slater, and I'm pleased to meet you".

He said, "Estil." It occurred to me that we may as well be family. I felt like kin already.

Estil turned, and we both went up onto the porch and through the weathered pine framed screen door into a neatly kept plain sixteen foot square room, a kitchen and (I'll call it) a recreation room-bedroom combination. "What a comfortable home," I observed. "I wish I could keep my house as well organized as you've done."

I think I stumped Estil, because he stopped for at least 5 seconds, and then he said gently, "Wife and dog are gone. Been gone for...forever. It seems like that." Then, he looked at me, a straight gaze, "She kept it clean...showed me how to keep up. It worked. For me." Estil leaned to reach into a little refrigerator about the size of my microwave oven. He pulled out a jug of water like a magician pulls a rabbit out of a hat, and set it down carefully, sitting down at his little cocktail sized table.

"Where do you get your water?" I asked, as I sat down on the other chair.

"Carry it up. Got a good spring down yonder." I poured out a pint into a clean jelly jar and took a long, refreshing swig.

"That's good...tasty." Estil poured a half glass and drank with me. "Jelly jars?" I asked.

"Uh huh," and a nod. "Guess so. Had 'em for...(silently counting) years." More silence and body language.

"Is this poverty?" I gathered up enough courage to risk it.

"Huh?" Estil looked right at me. "What you think? Why you thinkin' I'm poor? Yeah, I ain' got a big place or nothin'. Am I livin' in poverty?"

I felt a little regret (and embarrassment) about my question. "It's whatever you say," I responded. "Lots of people disagree. But, government thinks they need to get into it to protect people who don't have much."

"Protect them from what?" he asked.

"Oh, there are little old ladies who don't have a goat or a spring. Some couldn't walk down the hill or climb back up hauling a bucket. The government takes some of the money we send them at tax time and sends it to people who need it for food and other things."

Estil and I chatted like old fishing buddies for an hour. I could sense he was thinking about the future, when he would have to face up to his capability to handle the goat and the spring. I learned about Estil's support system. His daughter comes up out of her comfortable townhouse in Buckhannon with what amounts to a stack of newspapers and a week's rations. Estil trades extra goat's milk for a few essentials brought by his pal at the Salvation Army store. Sometimes, there are special treasures like boots and tarps and a sharp axe.

Sometimes, a book. I learned that some years, he can run his apples through an "Armstrong" press to make about forty gallons of cider. Some years yield only half as much. Cider trades for bean soup and fruit pie. It's an equal trade for some other goodies, too. Before she succumbed to a chronic disease, Estil's wife Lou made bread twice a week, and she was generous with her recipe and time spent teaching him (and lots of neighbors). So, baked goods are legitimate trading chips, too.

Does Estil own the land he lives on? Yes, it's family land with a hundred year history, and a very small real estate tax assessment gets paid on time twice each year. There's not much of value on his eight acres except the spring and his marginally fertile vegetable garden. The house is just two rooms, one all purpose room and one "utility" room, both nicely maintained by a man of dignity.

I wanted to prove to myself that poverty isn't a government-defined line on an income spreadsheet, and Estil reminded me that poverty doesn't have to be a money thing. I tried to boil down my notes to see if anything fit into a non-money pattern. In a motel room in Beckley, West Virginia, I made my conclusion: People who are clones of my new friend Estil don't live in poverty. They have assembled havens of comfort and safety by using assets within their little unique universes. Estil didn't wait around nor assume his condition constituted an entitlement. Within his capabilities, he gets busy every day, he maintains the condition of his little place, he thinks about tomorrow, and he participates like a good neighbor, both with family and with friends. It occurred to me that Estil never waits for someone else to take responsibility for situations that are clearly his business. He takes personal responsibility for every element of his eighty one year old life to the best of his limited ability. Estil Wendt earns the equivalent of $3,500 a year in the value of food and other benefits of barter and good will from his daughter and friends. For this man, it's about personal responsibility.

Chapter 9..................Instinct, Intuition, Psychology

There are interest groups who want to shape your understanding of poverty. They have motives you should know and understand, but just be aware that I have a motive, too. My motive is to put up a barrage of facts and evidence about poverty so I can sleep at night. I'm so aggravated by straw men and misdirected story lines that I'm compelled to put up a fight. There are power grabbers and vote sellers who are homing in on your scent. You've been targeted by lots of interest groups who are offering you candy and rides in their cars. They've enlisted ingenious publicity agents to get your attention and convince you to buy, contribute, volunteer, donate, submit, join the spirited mob, and comply. They're betting that they can enlist your sympathy and get you onto the anti-poverty train waving the flag of "balance the income" and "redistribute the wealth." In their quiver are the arrows of revolution and anarchy. There's the carbon shafted arrow of racial divide and there are media allies with baseless accusations against you and your demographic. The straw issue of poverty may have become one of the most effective enlistment tools available to sucker millions into joining the lemming army of wannabe occupiers. Worldwide calls to mount a campaign of hatred against income inequality and the wealth divide have been sounded, and unfortunately, vulnerable ears have heard the call. Have you figured out what their next ideological step might be?

You and I were affected more or less by fears of ridicule and rejection. Usually, teenage years are vulnerable to those bullys and beasts who make fun of your old fashioned hairstyle and your mismatched socks. For me, it was stripes and plaids. I don't ever remember caring about fitting into a clothes-defined social niche, but I'm sure I did. I'm aware of style bashing today because of family tales from the 1930s. My mother felt such incredible shame due to her home made flour sack clothing that she broke off her education in the eighth grade. She could have gone on to finish high school, but her embarrassment got the best of her.

It was about the perception of poverty. Even though there was always enough food and there was wood and coal for cooking and warmth, she was self conscious about her situation. Even though there was a nurturing social climate with fishing and baseball and obvious caring, funnelling part of her father's steady income into a clothing budget just didn't make it on his priority list. The antithesis of her ridicule and the shame she perceived showed up later in my mother's life as an excessive tendency to buy as much stylish clothing, shoes, and accessories as she could sneak into the house.

I've concluded that lots of people have perceptions of *culture-specific poverty* in Western civilization, fears that don't need to exist. My mother's family wasn't "poor," but she was exasperated to tears (and she surrendered to accept a short-circuited, insufficient education) because she thought her family was poor.

Embarrassment, low self esteem, anxiety, surrender, and depression give birth to envy and to behaviors that mask and compensate in what seem to be insane ways. Are you having neurotic responses to what you perceive to be your own condition of poverty? Do you feel vulnerable and at risk?

If circumstances put you into a lower income situation, how will you handle your fixed monthly commitments? Will you surrender, or will you get busy and wrestle your way back to a stable condition of positive cash flow? Who will you hold responsible for your twist, and who will be responsible for straightening things out?

Chapter 10............Poverty and Income Inequality

The world's brotherhood of macro-economists is a-twitter about *income inequality* as the new recently discovered economic miracle phrase. Income inequality is like a badge of pride unleashed to a world of fools, shinier than Alfred Nobel's prize and slicker than Karl Marx's pomade. It's refreshing to hear from such famous men of intelligentsia that an impoverished soul having no money has none due to the detestable existence of someone else who has lots. And, the disparity is worsening at a horrible avalanching rate. Specifically, $r > g$. The rate of capital return will out distance economic growth, thereby tipping the world's money cart right into the olympic sized swimming pools belonging to rich guys.

So economic poverty, what's left after the lake of money is drained by capitalists, is inevitable.

If you're an ostrich. I'm not content to take a snapshot of the looming inequality train wreck and tape it to the refrigerator, though, just so we can continue to despair over r and g. I'm an afficianado of what really happens in free markets unfettered by dictators, pretend dictators, and by media influenced by pretend macro-economists. So, my photo of the future includes producers, buyers, sellers, negotiators, consolidators, volunteers, consumers, employers, employees, partners, investors, all free to do what they do. My photo of each successive tomorrow has pictures of more and more individuals who get the message about the importance of taking personal responsibility for their lives, and they take it.

Because poverty isn't just a money thing. It's a condition, and you're in charge of your own unique one of a kind condition.

Chapter 11...............................Caution

This morning I became interested in American poverty after reading an AP story entitled "New gauge shows 49.7 million poor". Author Hope Yen refers to how old data, revised definitions, and new assumptions have been run up the flagpole. Her article leads me to suspect that either poverty is skyrocketing in America or our measuring stick is being manipulated by agenda pushers at the Washington D.C. Stretchers and Squeezers Club.

Why is computation of a "poverty level" important? It's the basis for 139 Federal and state government aid programs. Poverty level is the trigger mechanism for channeling 1.3 trillion dollars of borrowed U.S. Treasury dollars each year. So, the "level" number is a key to birthing the largest welfare economy in the world. The U.S. Treasury doesn't contain 1.3 trillion dollars. In fact, it never has. Today, the total welfare outflow is funded by IOUs with an insincere "I'll pay you Tuesday" note attached. This "borrow and spend" economic travesty is ingrained beneath a blanket of arrogance that stifles small voices of ethics and empirical sense. Virtually everyone who cares about economic justice knows the debt will never be paid off. That paradox leads me to a duality that concludes (1) everyone does not care, and (2) the jury dealing out economic justice is crooked. This duality is none other than the hypocrite rogue posing in Robin Hood's green tunic (another essay).

It's time to unstifle the voices. A compassionate culture is aware of the needs of incapacitated Americans and it upholds a discipline that motivates idle workers to become productive. But, remember, when we find the actionable root of the problem of poverty, it will be clear that poverty itself is an effect, not a cause.

Of course, poverty is not the only effect of cultural abandonment. And that's the whole point...an avalanche of other detrimental effects is triggered by a government that exercises complacency or corrupts cultural foundations.

Chapter 12..........................Swiss Cheese

With family status being one of the Federal factors determining who qualifies for poverty-based welfare, it's easy to trick the welfare system into thinking families with young adults are really separate individuals, each on a separate tab. If there is a wage earner, he or she supports all the rest, who are officially impoverished and needy, submitting multiple claims for assistance. According to news accounts that break through media protective filters, not only are unscrupulous welfare claimants crafty and bold, but bureaucratic defenses against this kind of fraud are swiss cheese. If you're one of the taxpayers who cares about fraud, I'm with you. If you're one of the shady welfare jostlers, continue and read further and pay special attention to chapters devoted to the root cause of poverty, where you can find some tips on helping to soften the fall for yourself and an avalanching mass of impoverished Americans. Please look.

Stealing from our treasury accentuates all of our poverty risks. Income tax fraudsters steal, but the ones who are not caught, adjudicated, and made to make restitution ultimately suck away at our reserves. People who lie their way to birth certificates, drivers' licenses, social security numbers, credit cards, mortgage loans, and bad checks diminish our culture and our piggy banks. In the end, you yourself are responsible for law enforcement by seeing to provisions for effective policing.

Chapter 13......Morality and Poverty

I suspect that the moral relativists are the same ones who assume poverty exists but has no root cause. To them, poverty is just another "woe" on the scale of woes, like 90 degrees is above 32 degrees on a thermometer. It "just is." In an environment disenfranchising morality, poverty is no more than a topic for talking points loaded into an M16, ready to shoot down detractors.

We're going to discover the root cause of poverty. Our discovery will be made by people who understand how financial health and personal responsibility intertwine. But to the relativist, root causes are like 13 round clips. They have no earthly function in a caring culture. Problems are simply problems, and they come from problem people: capitalists, Christians, police, the wealthy, the high wage earners...those are the source of all the problems according to relativists, the unfortunate captains who decided to abandon the compass and sextant.

So, the relativists' win-win is to accuse, adjudicate, judge, find guilty, and punish those capitalists, Christians, police, wealthy, and high wage earners. The win-win outcome is beautiful, because the public relations points are golden when the media perp-walks one dirty capitalist, those hypocritical Christians, one crooked policemen, those filthy rich arrogante, and those show-off workaholic high wage earners. Real crooks like Bernie Madoff, pediphile priests, and corrupt cops cut the knees from under good people, and the public eats up the soap opera message.

But, the relativists' thread of logic is built on an imaginary foundation. Fortunately, though, there *is* a root cause of poverty. It's a simple cause that can be divined and solved.

The root cause of poverty was born out of the twentieth century war to disavow morality, and the perpetrators of this war on morality are the people who want every behavior to be judged relative to other behaviors. It goes like this: an apple is better than a nut, a nut is better than a flat tire, and a flat tire is better than calling a man a terrorist. Calling a man a terrorist is better than starving a child, and starving a child is better than bullying twenty children. Bullying twenty children is better than eating broccoli...and so on. There is no "worst" behavior...just behaviors that are (in someone's opinion) better or worse. Nothing is absolutely the worst. Who is wise enough to judge what is the absolute worst? No one. Relativism is better, they say, and curiously, relativists judge absolutism to be absolutely bad without being able to imagine the hypocrisy in doing so.

On the other hand lots of Western religions assert there are moral absolutes. In fact, the absolutes are necessary in order to navigate civilization's climb out of barbarism. One famous modern day absolutist Peter Kreeft (A Refutation of Moral Relativism) writes that there are four cardinal pillars of morality: justice, courage, prudence, and self control. Kreeft's stand on absolutism stacks up very well in the challenge to find if the relativist's approach to morality could be infecting the root cause of poverty.

Why have governments stepped in to redistribute wealth? Don't they know when they attempt to move some people away from poverty that act brings others nearer to poverty? Where is the justice in that? When citizens perceive that they are entitled to something and then deprived of it, they sometimes try mob influence. Standing up to insurrection demands courage. It's the moral man's imperative. Giving in and buying an escape with other people's money strikes me as cowardly and ultimately immoral.

Forget my argument if you don't need a dose of morality to make you feel good. But, consider the weakness in the source of the moral relativist's point of view. Relativism was conceived as a mask for a guilty conscience...an indulgence. Relativism discards the concept of good and evil, and it overcomes the constricting ethical conundrum of God's commandments.

The rush of relief for people wishing to step outside the barbed wire of morality is a free and clear escape when "everybody's doing it". No strings, no aftertaste, no parents snooping outside your bedroom door. But, to disarm the mass indulgence-seeking army of moral relativists, there has to be big artillery and massive culture shifts. The battle to eradicate poverty depends on enlisting you and other Americans to man a front line stand against morality's disintegration. And, I believe victory in this war will bring poverty to its knees.

Chapter 14 ....Handy and Rose

Handy and Rose met in high school when athletes floated through the halls on pedestals and sixteen year old girls fantasized about quarterbacks and convertible cars. Handy was a halfback/quarterback/utility man on a high energy football team with a mediocre record. Like all the "also ran" high school football teams, GHS boosters liked to focus on the few successes and downplay defeats. So did the Sophomore girls. Rose focused on Handy's icon status and he noticed her attentiveness. They were the high school sweethearts who went on to marry and let fate carry them from one apartment to another, while Handy ricocheted from one entry-level job to another.

Both Rose and Handy made the marriage promise, but Handy forgot his promise shortly after their second baby was born. He was missing in action more than once, but he survived and came home with inventive stories. Rose had trouble believing the stories, and when rumors crippled her ability to trust her husband, she sent him to the dog house, whereupon Handy took his letter jacket and the laptop computer and ran off with paralegal-in-training Louise to Cincinnati.

Grandmas and grandpas always relent when a daughter like Rose knocks on the door with such a dilemma that includes grandbabies, and that's the way the story went. Within three days, Rose was working for a local maid service cleaning other people's homes for minimum wage. Grandma baby-sat, and Rose started working a second job, the evening shift at Fresh Market as a cashier. She sold her fifteen year old car and walked to work except in bad weather, when her father shuttled her back and forth. After saving for a year, Rose moved herself and the children to a little cottage, and took in a boarder, a 60 year old widow lady who was willing to baby-sit in return for rent. Rose never stopped searching for better situations so her two children could know unconditional love from a mother who was willing to adapt and sacrifice.

Handy and Louise lived it up during their eighteen month fling, until

Cincinnati landlords figured out they couldn't rent to people who didn't pay the second month's rent, or the third, or the fourth. Handy signed up for work as a car dealership wash and prep man, as an apprentice in the Pipefitter's and Welder's Union, as a utility man in a suburban cafeteria, as a house painter, as a bricklayer's helper, as a janitor in a middle school, and as an insurance adjuster trainee. No job lasted one full week because Handy neglected to disclose to any of the potential employers about his illness. He was sick every day. He was sick of getting up, sick of getting to work on time, and sick of calling in sick. "No show" Handy Handmacher made himself quite a reputation in blue collar Cincinnati. With an imaginative mind and Louise's assistance, Handy worked through the application processes for seven State of Ohio and Hamilton County welfare entitlements due to his extreme poverty situation. Handy is now talking with lawyers who specialize in workmen's compensation claims to get financial relief for a back injury he suffered when working briefly as a house painter.

Instead of buying bread and milk, Handy rushes to the most convenient store where scratch-off retirement plans are sold. His results so far would cause the odds-makers to conclude Handy's retirement is a long shot.

After a year and a half as a single mom, Sarah "Rose" Rosebaum Handmacher and her two children are self sufficient, living on her income from two jobs. Her gross income is $1,700 a month, and she's saving about $100 a month so she can buy a car. She has not applied for any assistance, but she is compelled to pay $75 a month for a subsidized health care policy that covers her and her children.

Chapter 15....................Diluting Responsibility

Social togetherness, interaction for common good, community cooperatives, neighborhood organizations, and democracy itself are ways to disseminate and improve understanding of common risks and community needs. Teams with diverse representation have found that genuine improvements and ingenius products can come from group planning and decision making. Working together advances all the partners.

An unfortunate feature of group invention and decision making is that individuals tend to feel the distribution of responsibility for the final results statistically removes them from any significant liability if something goes wrong. Blame for failure diminishes, because the other members of the group (theoretically) carry their substantial percentage of it. There's a feeling of individuals being spotlighted for success, but having no responsibility for failure. In a similar line of thinking, this is the same reason individuals participating in flash thievery mobs get away with a low probability of blame or being held responsible.

There's another responsibility-shirking way to multiply strength of results and divide blame for individual weaknesses. It's collective bargaining. Hiring a front man to advocate for a client group is a popular way to spread out the gritty end of the negotiating stick. It's like putting eggs into a community basket and hoping for a smooth trip. Coordinated actions to motivate negotiators (strike threats) are available, and they're legitimate according to Federal regulations. This seemingly extortion-like tactic is available to be used by labor organizations, and it is upheld and enforced by the National Labor Relations Board. Ducking behind a technicality is abandonment of responsibility, to me.

Striking workers tend to believe that none of the responsibility for broken delivery promises, sales interruptions, financial losses, or bankruptcy drop through to them. At their level as individual employees, dilution of blame is as good as a reprieve. The opposite of responsibility dilution is the doctrine of "everyone's responsible", as is the case in environmental law, where the entire liability for an environmental disaster can be assessed to one polluter (joint and several liability), even though his contribution to the debacle might have been a small percentage of the total.

Who or what is responsible for American poverty? In order to justify my claim that "individual failure to accept personal responsibility" is the lowest common denominator and the root cause of poverty, let me refer you to the chart of "Signatures of Personal Responsibility". Then, let's think this through.

If you lost your job and you have bills and other liabilities leaving you at poverty's front door, get another job (anything with regular income) and slash your spending. Unburden yourself from fixed costs (mortgage, car payment) by selling those assets that won't disappear by themselves. Sacrifice enough to bring your spending down to a number below your new income. It's up to you and your personal responsibility pedigree.

If your lifestyle drains so much of your income that you can see poverty hurtling toward you, pull back on the throttle. Put on the brakes. Have the courage to take control. It's all you.

If you can't find a place to get a job, you're probably not trying (or you're looking for a slot where your expectations are masking the reality of your experience level). Loosen up and take a week to become a job market genius. There are last resorts, too, like Manpower and Kelly Services. Get a pair of work gloves and tell them you'll do any job that's available. You might have to be willing to relocate temporarily so you can work your way back up the experience/pay scale. If you do, temporarily whittle your expenditures so your piggy bank will put on some weight. Someday, you'll have more bacon and less fat. You're the only one who can open the employment office door. You're responsible. It's you who has to take a mighty grip on your paycheck. Just you.

Are you tempted to indulge in some of those behaviors that steal your money? You're probably giving in because you've let some mind-altering thief into your head or into your life. It's time to knuckle down with a can of high horsepower courage (like V-8) and summon all your bravado. Kick those things that have convinced you to cower like a little puppy. Reject the temptation to throw your paycheck into the "fast and loose" trash can. If there's family, do it for them. You and you having your own way are two of the most selfish and least important things in the world. Be strong. Be responsible for the gift of strength God and your parents entrusted you with.

Chapter 16.............Teaching Personal Responsibility

The curriculum for a basic degree in Personal Responsibility consists of three main topics, courage, self esteem, and decision making. Think about the people you know who have risen into professional careers where taking personal responsibility is a fundamental requirement. These pop into my mind:

- Architect
- Surgeon
- Air Traffic Controller
- EMT Emergency Medical Technician
- Battlefield Medic
- Air Transport Pilot
- Nuclear Plant Operator
- Nanny

What qualifies all these occupations for a high score on the personal responsibility scale? All have human safety (and life and death) hanging in the balance. All these job holders have "clients" whose expectations are paramount. Each job requires a holder to step up, step in, and take charge when the situation arises, and it's clear that stepping up is a signature of courage and dedication to doing what needs to be done. But, personal responsibility pertains to mundane little situations, too, like doing household chores and bushing your teeth. Stepping up can simply be getting yourself down to the market when the baby needs milk, and it can be as complicated and difficult as calling that meeting to announce to your employees that the plant is closing. So, there are varying degrees of courage involved in taking personal responsibility, but abandoning the easy chair is a pretty common prerequisite.

"C.J." was a good dad. He went right to work after serving in the Navy as an apprentice mechanic in a local auto repair shop. He kept telling his police patrolman pal that he'd like to be on the city's law enforcement team, and during a period of a slim labor market in our little town, C.J. was hired onto the ten man police force. He took a certain pride in being a rookie, and he worked his way up the ladder over a twenty year period. He was steadfast and strong. He took his job seriously, and he carried principles of personal ethics with him everywhere he went. Here's the personal responsibility story that has always stuck in my mind: C.J. was my step father. Our family would take a little drive on lots of weekends, and the purpose was strictly "sightseeing," although sometimes we'd end up at Grandpa and Grandma's house at the exact time they made popcorn or ate ice cream. One evening, we drove (dad was the driver) to the "five points" intersection at the same time some hot rod teenager squealed (recklessly) to a stop at the cross street, revving his engine like a drag racer. Without hesitating, my dad put our car in neutral and pulled the emergency brake. He quickly and with an air of focus walked up to the teenage driver's door and gave a dramatic order to roll down the window. Then, dad gave this kid the kindest no-nonsense safety exhortation I've ever heard. The teenager shrank to about 3 feet tall and tucked his ego away. He was shocked by a man (my dad) whose thought was to save his life and the lives of other motorists. My dad always had the courage to take personal responsibility for doing what was right, and the everyday lessons he gave made his mission clear without using the police badge as his claim to authority. I've thought about the people I've known over the years, and my step father gets my "strength through kindness and courage" award. Later, I realized it was about taking personal responsibility as a duty to help others.

In addition to courage, self esteem plays a role in the personal responsibility recipe. Knowing you have a good chance of success opens the way to start moving toward an objective. Actually, *believing* you have at least a glimmer of a chance is what it takes sometimes to propel you past the "help wanted" sign and to take the initiative to give your best effort in a job interview. With self esteem, your confidence in yourself shows through clearly.

Employers like that.

Self esteem can't be bought. It has to be developed through a long process that includes support and encouragement from others, usually your parents. The process of building self esteem is complicated, but I know it includes celebrating your successes (however small) and patiently repairing the aftermath of your failures (even the big ones). The sum total of all these experiences builds over a lifetime, and at some time along the way, taking personal responsibility for your own life becomes intuitive.

Decision making is a skill that's learned through important lessons out in the world (experience), because great decisions depend on finding facts and evaluating real possibilities. One decision making process emphasizes finding experts with the facts and including their input. Good decision making always requires clearly defining the objective to be met when deploying your decision. Sometimes, making a decision has to be split second, and there are lots of fire and rescue stories that exemplify split second decision making. Some decisions have to be made with care, because they have to be right the first time. They may take a long time, because being right counts in making decisions that affect lots of lives or impact big ticket commitments.

Blaming others for your own failures creates a bad scenario for them and for you. Holding yourself responsible for your decisions, your actions, and what you regard as your duty is seen by others as the sign of a real man (or woman). Taking credit for your own successes might be bragging, but "if you've done it, you can brag about it." You'll be able to sleep at night and you can smile when you wake up.

Chapter 17......................Coffee at Jasper's

When the big round clock told us it was ten oclock, I thought the twelve chairs we filled would fit right up front by Jasper's (Cafe) front window, where we could see and be seen. This was my day to collect poverty horror stories from residents who lived here near the intersection of Poplar and Front. I offered coffee and muffins for all comers, and Elaine (at Jaspers) made good on my request. For a while, anyhow. By eleven-thirty, we had forty-one coffee and muffin enthusiasts, and Elaine was bringing in cookies from the Save-a-Lot in order to satisfy. The coffee flowed, and so did orange juice, milk, Pepsi, and...well, anything else anyone called for. It would have been more than a two hundred dollar rap session (plus a $40 tip), if I hadn't pulled up stakes before noon.

I asked every passer-by on Tuesday morning to pass the word about the session I was hosting on Wednesday, and I'd say no one got disappointed. On Tuesday, I asked the gal at Jaspers if she'd be prepared for a mass invasion on Wednesday, and she gave a smiley "yes". "Lunch time might be tight, though", she warned. I said we'd wrap it up before noon.

I paid $80 for a high end digital voice recorder on Ebay, and I recorded the entire hour and forty-five minutes of our "Jasper's Cafe" event. I took notes, too, but I've listened to the whole rap session recording at least ten times, now. I tried to remember all the names of the people (mostly ladies) who came through the door, but frankly, only a few names stuck in my memory. There was Adrian, Pick (short for Pickles), ZZ, May-sha, Ma, and more who seemed to have nicknames. There were elderly, middle aged, children, and two gentlemen who I remember clearly, Arzwell and James.

"Good morning, and thank you for coming to Jasper's to help me find problems in low income zones. Problems that need to be fixed. It's about not being able to have enough at bill-pay time. It's about having to do with less. If you don't mind, I'm going to try to write down short bullets here on my easel pad so I can remember...words to help me put it all together. Here's one, <u>We don't have a car that works</u>." I jotted <u>car trouble</u> on the pad. Then the flood gate opened. Here's a condensed list.

- Car trouble
- Can't go to Costco (car)
- Food costs more at convenience store
- Laundromat not easy
- Ride the bus too long
- Bill collectors hassle
- Check cashing fee
- Bill paying adds 10%
- Late fees eat up too much
- Cash advance costs 15% -7 days
- Depressed and disgusted
- Rent goes up
- Blood donation is hassle
- Getting robbed
- Too much pay to qualify for subsidies
- Discouraged in job hunt
- Can't fill out applications-help
- Low pay
- Job competition
- Too much police or not enough
- No community building or pool
- Mail boxes get broken into
- Hot water not hot
- Leaks

When time was up, I thanked all for being present, but only a few got up to leave. "Our time's up, but if you have some more thoughts, here's how you can call me or email. For the next week, I'm going to think through these problems, and try to see if there are answers. If you'd like, we could come back here in a week for another meeting. Who would show up?" Almost every hand shot up. Hmmm. I'll have to talk to Jasper's about how to do this for less than two hundred dollars. I wonder if a second session could harvest some really great grass roots ideas? Then, I yelled (to the diminishing group), "Everybody write down a couple of ideas in the next week that would knock out some of these problems." I was pretty much ignored in the rush. I folded up my easel and chart pad with 4 pages of ink and words. I turned off my recorder and fled the scene after paying Elaine.

At home, I tried to dream up some ways to elicit solutions to this list of problems next week, but I kept thinking I'd get a lot of easy answers, none of which would validate my conclusion.

I did go back to Jasper's, but only with one question, "Who didn't take the responsibility for getting these problems fixed?" My panel of two dozen in the second week session unanimously blamed someone else, never themselves for each of their situations. I guess on the surface, my experiment was a big zero, but what I learned was that people near the poverty line have been conditioned somehow to expect someone else to take responsibility for all their social and financial problems. Where did they get that idea? I want individuals to take personal responsibility for all aspects of their lives, because I believe that's the way to fix poverty. The unconditioning process looks like it will be my first real challenge.

Chapter 18.........Dean "Ocean" (O'Shay), Reno, Nevada

Four of us flew into Reno, Nevada as our hopping off point to visit Lake Tahoe and Yosemite National Park. All those plans worked just fine, and a week later, we drove back to Reno to explore for a day and a half prior to flying home. From my award winning (I've been awarded the "most judgmental man in the world" plaque) point of view, Reno is a little pile of dirt where none of the "Westward Ho" crowd stopped to plant seeds of Methodism or to drive a Quaker stake. If legalized gambling and the frilly magnets didn't exist, all the men of iron and steel would have kept the conestoga motors running, and they would have kept going west.

I met Dean. Dean drove his Mazda up to Reno some unrememberable number of years ago and he decided to stay. There was Dean O'Shay in the (mostly empty) parking lot at the Atlantis Reno Resort Casino, with the Mazda hood up. Now, I'm not a certified diagnostician, but I've held hands with all the millimeter Snap-ons and every miraculous Vise Grip, and I couldn't just walk on by. I don't know what the car's real problem was, but I remember Dean's real problem.

Dean was stuck between two fantasy lives. One was the steady, stable life of a high school graduate driving a milk bulk truck in Red Oak, Iowa and the other was that of a blackjack king, living a compensated lifestyle in the casino hotel tower. But, reality forced Dean to live in his car, and the living didn't look too good to me. Right now, Dean and his battery didn't have have that spark.

"Need some help?" He had a pounded down in the dirt and defeated look.

"No, thanks," was the short version. When I didn't hurry away, he asked "Got jumper cables?"

"No...well I don't think so, I'm driving a rental car. But if that'll do it, let's go get some at Walmart. I've got time on my hands." Dean hesitated.

When I convinced Dean I wasn't a mugger or a pervert, he let me buy a round of Subway sandwiches at a plaza a couple of blocks away. As we sat down, he said, "Jumpers probably wouldn't fix the problem more than once, I've got 'ta move around...it's probably time for me to head for California."

I stared at my 6" cold-cut sub and asked, "Why not Iowa?"

It was a quiet 10 seconds, but he admitted, "Nah. There's nothing. I've just got to get into the groove."

Dean seemed to still have hope for a jackpot that would just jump into his pocket. He hadn't mortgaged his positive attitude, but I'll bet he will. It was a huge struggle to keep my mouth shut, so I didn't blurt out, "You ought to straighten up and go get a real job. You know you'd be better off. You're wasting your time, and you're falling right into other people's plans to take your food money." Who knows? Maybe he'd take advice from the guy who just paid for his sub.

"You get SNAP? Food stamps?" I asked. "That ought to keep you going 'til something better comes along."

"Well, yeah, but it's hard to get your car fixed with food stamps."

"Is there family back where you lived?" No answer. I'ts probably a bad thing to bring up. So, I told him my story. "My wife and I have 4 kids and 7 grandchildren. My wife and I went to see Yosemite. We're here with our travelling buddies, Phil and Sharon, and right now, they're over there feeding the slots." Then, I breathed a little, while Dean worked over his empty sub wrapper, picking up the little lettuce shreds. I think he just ran out of conversation, and his drift was toward getting back on the hunt for casino gold.

I thought I might be able to do something useful by asking about the age of his Mazda battery. I asked, "Car batteries from 5 to 7 years old die of old age, usually...could yours be real old?"

He breathed out a sigh and "Yeah." Just that.

I dropped Dean off at the Atlantis parking lot, and he just waved me off. I think he had a plan, but it didn't include me driving him to NAPA and shelling out a hundred dollars for a battery. I parked and hurried inside to find my wife and friends. I did, and I was happy no one lost more than a few bucks on the slots. I didn't play, so I won.

My brief encounter with Dean made me think he's not just unlucky, he's trying unsuccessfully to bury some old skeleton in a shallow hole. I'd say he didn't listen to his grandma or his mother, who told him to "Do whatever you have to do to take good care of yourself and your family." I know one of them told him, because all grandmas and moms say that. Dean "Ocean" O'Shay couldn't hack the job of taking personal responsibility for his own life. He took a flying leap at success, but when he found out the improbability of being dealt a hold-em royal flush to bolster his own dream, he didn't believe the odds were 64,974 to 1, so his back-to-the-wall ego kept playing. It still forces him to play away what's left of every check the taxpayers send. Gambling is not the cause of Dean's condition, because gambling can't make decisions and kick an addiction. Dean's in charge of his fix, and so far, he has failed to take personal responsibility to get out.

Chapter 19.....Saying "No" to Poverty

So your payday and your spending can't seem to live as friends? Is your financial condition on the edge of a cliff at the end of every month? Is there a credit card with payment demands that seem to be stripping you to the bone? Does the bill collector of Christmas past scare you into hiding when the doorbell rings? Sounds like you need some "say no" lessons.

You could "say no and mean it" by confronting all those temptations that are being secreted by your swollen ego. You might confess that most of your discretionary spending is for useless junk, and you could practice walking away. Have a candid discussion with yourself and see if you understand your temptations. Separate your mind's view of your "stuff" from your "self." Admit that your toys do not define you...not really.

Could you change your spending style over night? Who would be responsible for doing that?

Chapter 20.........Other Effects of the "One Cause" Claim

I've acknowledged there is a narrow little list of candidates that can claim to be in line to be called the *single* root cause of poverty, and there's a reason that cause is elusive in many camps. Poverty's one root cause also is the cause of a staggering number of cases of hunger, personal bankruptcy, health deterioration, delinquency, divorce, and uncountable other personal failures. The one root cause of poverty is *personal irresponsibility.*

Personal responsibility is the virtue that trumps all other human interventions working to overcome poverty. Consider the father who gets out of bed early for his shot at honest hard work where he can earn an honest day's pay. Consider how and why that father could look for work or make a job of selling his own creative services. Consider how he could start early and stay late to earn dignity as well as a payday. Consider the single mom who could integrate care for her babies in her plan and still provide a useful service or situation of employment. Think about the couple that budgets and plans for the family's necessities, sustenance, water, shelter, warmth. They're the people who think and search to learn alternatives for success. Envision the degree of sacrifice family providers have to adapt to and obstacles they must overcome. Picture the hard work and the sweat. Picture a sigh of relief at the end of one of those days of labor. Imagine the pride.

Chapter 21...............Popular Solutions to Poverty

Why do the popular media-ready solutions to poverty all sneak the concept of "free money" into headlines? Let's see. Anti-poverty pop culture loves "debt forgiveness." Debt forgiveness sounds great for the debtor, the person who stands to shake that darn bankruptcy trap and those harrassing phone calls. Imagine too, creditors could get a wonderful feel-good glow by Faxing over a philanthropic "Paid in Full" receipt. What generosity! Or, what if all the big banks just sent out debt forgiveness letters? Those fat cats could just "do it." What's wrong with that?

All employers ought to guarantee full employment. No layoffs, no firing unneeded employees. And, full 40 hour weeks for everyone. Free medical insurance and golden retirement plans would have to be offered, too. Companies that balk could be fined or taxed, and their greedy CEOs could be thrown into jail. That'd fix their money grubbing wagons!

Landlords ought to be prohibited from evicting tenants. After all, there's no humane reason to throw renters out into the snow, into life and death situations. Families must not be made to suffer mental anguish nor physical danger due to eviction.

Free cellphones were given to millions of low income people so they could call potential employers to seek work. Also, Human Relations departments could call potential employees (who have free phones) and invite them to fill job vacancies. Of course, free cellphone plans would make sense, too, because who can use a free phone if they can't pay for minutes? This sounds like a great way to enable an unemployed person to get a job. It's a win-win.

The logic of giving free cellphones makes me realize that free transportation and a free suit would help put the unemployed back to work, too. Am I rolling? This fight against poverty really is fun!

Really? These ideas must have been dreamed up by idiots and thieves. I imagine letting all convicted felons out of jail would be good, too. They could augment our job market, and gross domestic product would grow like crazy. I'm joking, of course, but there are people who have not thought through these economically insane solutions to reducing (not enough money) poverty. Why are there islands of insanity out there? You know. Or, at least you suspect there are answers in the old chest of drawers where jealousy and envy are stored. Moses brought a clue when his commandment on coveting other people's property came down. "Thou shalt not steal" rings a bell with me. Any forcible wealth redistribution or outright theft from a legitimate owner is wrong. Every contract carries weight, and every commitment deserves dutiful fulfillment. Banks manage other people's money, and very little of their own, so debt forgiveness would avalanche down to steal from depositors who have legitimate ownership of bank funds.

The whole idea of apartment leasing and rental of living quarters is for an entrepreneur to provide homes for renters choosing not to buy their own. Risk takers who invest and upgrade living quarters for renters do so with an expectation of compensation, and renters have a right to expect value for their rental buck. There's a mutual understanding, a give and take, and fulfillment of a beneficial good. You need to realize that nothing in a free society is really free. There's no free money at the bank, no free apartment, and there's no free pass for robbing a liquor store. Those fantasies are not real. They're generated by envy-driven dreams, and to wait around expecting them to come true is a trademark of irresponsibility. No welfare check is written without an equal balancing withdrawal being made from someone's hard-earned paycheck.

Chapter 22 ....The Wrong Answers

So, throwing other people's (taxpayer's) money at the problem of poverty is foolish. Blaming straw factors for causing poverty (and hence creating straw targets) like inequality, capitalism, greed, and racism undermines useful progress and obscures the real foundation begging to be repaired. Redistributing fruits of honest hard workers to prop up irresponsibly maintained houses and to distribute charity food baskets for citizens who have abandoned responsibility is immoral. These acts of faux charity hurt both the giver and the recipient.

False Samaritans who tripwire your guilt and advocate for pieces of your hard earned pie need to be called out. Hypocritical pretend beggars and victimhood pimps who actually have no hunger or discomfort of their own, but who carry on public relations programs of fake charity just for publicity, fame, money, and votes defraud the creed of ethics a free society needs.

Capitalism, industry, and business are all usual suspects in the poverty finger pointing game, but indictments almost never ring true. More likely, the accuser is an enemy of big business bent on extortion and shake-down, or just a jealous community mob organizer wannabe. In other countries where competition has been squashed by dictates of a self serving oligarch, business, markets, and industry are at the whim of the ruling class. The businesses are at risk of impoverishment just like the population is poverty-prone. In a free market where competition is honored by all participants, and where a "subsidies for cronies and barriers to opponents" style of corruption is rejected, enterprises can generate commerce and jobs for everyone.

I absolutely reject the ideas that one race is uniquely destined for poverty and one race is uniquely responsible for other peoples' impoverishment. People of all races whose ancestors fell victim to generational mortgaging of freedoms and who failed to jump back up to persevere inevitable struggles have had to start their marathon runs to success later than some others. But, every run to the finish line is still exactly the same distance it has always been. The distance for all runners is miles of honest hard work over a course that requires avoiding pitfalls that snatch at personal responsibility.

Conclusion

I've convinced myself that poverty described as a culture-specific situation of individuals and families has one and only one root cause. *Failing to take personal responsibility* for life's challenges is the root cause of poverty. Except for physical and mental handicaps and out and out enslavement, there are no other cultural causes of poverty as fundamental. Every other reason for poverty that is held up to compete against *failure to take personal responsibility* is itself an effect of the same failure I've described.

Amishman Jacob Hochstetler immigrated to the U.S. From Switzerland in 1736 in order to live free of Swiss obligations he and his family disagreed with on religious terms. In 1757 Hochstetler's family was partly decimated by an Indian attack, but Jacob and two sons survived to go on to create a family with decendents numbering in the thousands. The spirit of taking personal responsibility has survived with the Amish in America since 1736, and their example is a legend in many parts of the country.

Estil Wendt grew up in Appalachia where "you took what God gave you, and you made it work." His way of life convinced me that the proverb etched on his wall "Instead of trying to get what you want, try to want what you've got" was connected to ancestral ethics carried down by farmers, dairymen, and lumbermen. Estil's simple unassuming ways certainly would inspire others who happened by for a short visit. Do your homework on goats, and he'll want to chat for an hour.

Dean O'Shay hadn't given up on hope when I met him in 2014. Unfortunately, he was hoping for a miracle that was less likely to come true than being struck by lightning. Dean's sure thing was poverty, both the money kind and the lifestyle kind. He could have cashed in on a big dose of family values and lessons in responsibility, had they been in the cards.

C.J. Metzger is one of my heroes, because he stepped up to commit to a lifetime as my step father (my mother's second husband), the solid rock replacement for my father who perished in the Pacific. C.J. was my role model as a man of personal ethics and honest hard work. I wish he were here today to mentor my children and grandchildren, too.

Jasper's Cafe's ad hoc committee didn't produce what I thought it would, but I think I learned plenty about who's to blame for situations related to poverty. I learned that "you" are the person most powerful to honcho the resolution of "your" problems. Blaming others is a cop-out.

Macro-economist Thomas Piketty (<u>Capital in the Twenty-First Century</u>) (2013), seems to have pulled the string on a party popper of chaff and fodder for pundits who want desperately to blame capitalism for any species of poverty whose DNA they can identify. I imagined one ecstatic Nobel economist in particular having to change his shorts when he read Piketty's "gotcha" essay. Despite statistics to back up Piketty's claim, I'm unable to see a causal relationship in the apples of poverty and the oranges of capitalism. I wish he'd look at capitalism as a dynamo of *anti-poverty* to see what adds up.

Moses is reputed to have brought down the commandments that include a caution against coveting thy neighbor's wife and his wealth. I'm giving Moses an A+ for a good try, but latter day paupers are feigning ignorance of the clay instructions. Envying other people's wealth is still way too popular.

Andrew "Handy" Handmacher's Achilles' heel was starting from scratch with no glimmer of behavioral or ethical standards to be learned from his absent father. In fact, Handy emulated almost every fault and failing his dad had shown the family twenty years earlier. For the Handmachers, the bridge linking family history to his present situation is still submerged in the proverbial Kwai.

Sarah "Rose" Rosebaum Handmacher in contrast, emulated her maternal grandmother, who worked 40 hours a week at an industrial job attending looms and spinning machines. Grandma was 65 when she retired, setting a 42 year example of honest hard work, a paid-in-full mortgage, and a retirement savings account that grew despite her grand excursion trip at the age of 68 to nine countries in Europe and the Middle East.

To: (undisclosed) County Welfare Board

Subject: Request for Immediate Cash Subsidy for a Person Way Below the Poverty Line

My rent keeps coming due month after month non-stop, and the landlord keeps harrassing me to pay for months that are already over and done with. The convenience store has made it so inconvenient to shop there, because they demand payment before my SNAP card gets replenished. My car won't run because when it's out of gas it's impossible to get it to the gas station. My ex-girlfriend stole my cell phone, so I can't contact employers. They can't contact me, either, but there aren't any job openings in my choice of career, anyway. High school was impossible to get through because all the high achievers skewed the curve. College would be a joke because of the crippling tuition costs nowadays. You can't get on American Idol or The Voice unless you already have 10,000 hours of practice. Power Ball numbers are impossible to guess, and little guys don't have a chance unless they buy thousands of tickets. The Food Line only serves one meal a day, and it's just food other people don't want to eat. What kind of sense does that make?

That's why it's impossible to get a new start in a job that pays enough to get by. I want to do more than just get by. I heard that people who expect nothing get nothing, so I'm expecting you to see my need and respond with generosity.

Sincerely,
   (name withheld)

Signature of Personal Responsibility

Says "No" to Wasteful Behaviors

- "No" Alcohol
- "No" Drugs
- "No" Gambling
- "No" Excesses
- "No" Lies
- "No" Abuse
- "No" Laziness
- "No" Lewdness
- "No" Arrogance
- "No" Vengeance
- "No" Hatefulness
- "No" Selfishness

Signature of Personal Responsibility

Maintains Steady Income from Honest Hard Work

- Meets or exceeds Job Expectations
- Honors Job Commitments
- Matches Job Hunt to Qualifications
- Accepts and Thrives on Competition
- Willing to Create a New Business
- Pays for What They Get and Insists on Getting What They Pay for.

Signature of Personal Responsibility

Makes Bold Promises and Keeps Them

- Budgets and Saves
- Avoids Deficits
- Makes Decisions with Long Term Vision
- Commits Truthfully to Love, Honor, and Obey in Sickness and in Health, Until Death
- Is Predictable and Reliable
- Minimizes Debt

Signature of Personal Responsibility

Prioritizes Family First

- Kindness Starts at Home
- Patience Starts at Home
- Acceptance Starts at Home
- Demonstrates Role Model Qualities
- Adopts and Shares Personal Principles
- Cares for Elderly Family

Signature of Personal Responsibility

Never Stops the Quest for Learning and Improving

- Seeks Additional Skills Training
- Maintains Social Immersion
- Seeks Creative Pastimes
- Willing to Experiment
- Seeks to Understand Civic Duty

Thank You

For the numerous stories that inspired me to arrange this jigsaw my way into one picture of hope and understanding, I'm grateful. For those who are still trying to figure out where the borders and the corners go, I'd love to be involved some more. Although poverty means different things to different people, there is pain and despair that deserves a chance of being fixed, and a dialogue about the elements that make full and permanent repairs possible cannot be bad.

It would be thrilling to find out someday that no American is without the life preserving staples of food, shelter, clothing, and well being that comfort and sustain our humanity. And, I'd be very happy to find that it's no longer interesting nor profitable to incite envy and poverty paranoia for selfish purposes.

In this endeavor, like all others, I'd like to recommend a relevant letter composed by a person whose counsel I respect greatly (and it reads): "If trouble plagues you, be patient and persistent, because patience and persistence are the qualities that build the strength of your character. It is in your character that there is hope."

Story details and names referred to in this book were selected by the author, and they may be real or fictional.

The author can be contacted via email at eeslater@engineer.com